whelmed

NICOLE MARKOTIĆ

Coach House Books | Toronto

first edition

Published with the generous assistance of the Canada Council for the Arts and the Ontario Arts Council. Coach House Books also acknowledges the support of the Government of Canada through the Canada Book Fund and the Government of Ontario through the Ontario Book Publishing Tax Credit.

LIBRARY AND ARCHIVES CANADA CATALOGUING IN PUBLICATION

Markotić, Nicole, author
    Whelmed / Nicole Markotić. -- First edition.

Poems.
Issued in print and electronic formats.
ISBN 978-1-55245-326-1 (paperback)

    I. Title.

PS8576.A7435W44 2016   C811'.54   C2015-908204-8

Whelmed is available as an ebook: ISBN 978 1 77056 447 3 (EPUB), 978 1 77056 448 0 (PDF), 978 1 77056 460 2 (MOBI)

Purchase of the print version of this book entitles you to a free digital copy. To claim your ebook of this title, please email sales@chbooks.com with proof of purchase or visit chbooks.com/digital. (Coach House Books reserves the right to terminate the free digital download offer at any time.)

for Louis Cabri

a-

bandon

to wild. wild, bodacious, bandit, and branded. a rear deposit, posited. trade for trade, and weary, and eerily, and -ily. give up colour and fluenced broadsides. this rag, this peppered snag. grasp the ladder and holes won't stream by. bandy-on, clever a-hoy. a-cling, a-stifle, a-stash. carry on, to the final creet coda. sneeze first, ask proposals anon

bashed

open wide! newly zinger alters. bad-ass away, and tributed. itials for every itiation. a-bow, a-bad, a-borrow, a-bumpkin. to serve, tect. ive and lative following. of to and not without, without. the green wunderkind stole the sibling dais. ages and ages

damant

not amant, nor positive pathos, nor forementioned. skivvy the hardest, most genitive iron. tame the undæmon, foreign to Greek. tame in time for breakfast, sixteen chin-ups for the lunch lady. sit one in. begin in front, then velope the article. mining fissures. the dame under the hat suited up. back, back, fill

ghast

antique ghosts, for sure! spooked when hasty and grovelling. hazmat horror, perfective frightening: tensive and a-tensive. flabbered, too. bed archaic wit, here. do not pee on the chesterfield, do not spit into the wind. I'm achuffed, four slurs! ahysterical much? do not fart sideways, do not. burp indoors, do not. hiccups hug the larynx, fairly. shall one betroth a bit of daunt? so crepit

lign

opposed to lienate / or at all avuncular. no pologies for French spelling. migraine polka Wednesday. start the hand-job rehearsal, his doppelgänger opts. *true dat*. this pathy menable to every moeba. ago, ago, anti dote

loof

plain weather-gauge; plainly Dutch. ship's distance, spare penny in the heel of her shoe. glut of anti-luft, with or without balloons, preferably crimson. bridged take on nautical agency. this just in: two jobs and you're out. forswore and forsooth. *so* morously. hoofwards leads foolproof, and zed-proof

noint

secretion-free secrations? bags and bags of oily rags. spersed smearing, from medicalized aholes, vout-wipings. though only when peeling in public, only when pointing to the uphill trail. torn and rippling sunder. one dweeb's partment, bedaub the wound, denervate the hand crank. bespeak!

plomb

to tender the plummet: asplash, averve, a fruit-shaped vogue. great, nificant, spot-on, and angled downward. wardward, with phlegm. leaning into sangfroid, lumbering over then around, rounding the tumble, umbling, blinginging. please, please yourself. shine for me. shiny blobs, mumba lobs. one plum. afright, aramble, aplus. plus this

propos

to the of: further jections. for toward and nearly, and gard. *en passant,* byway digressives. pure cidents, bare *uns,* whole swack of posals. as art deco brags, from geometric intrigues to sun-risen vices, so too

spirate

how you say beep's favoured drawl, minus the original shins. don't spire the notion, beep the nation, port cods or frankfurts to single ports. sporting bobbed apples. spit, alternating *in* and *in.* inbiased maternal ticulates. as in *hurry,* as in *hubba,* as in puff. the imagic tailed tale. *a hem*

sylum

negative seizure. sly lump, slippery radiance, sighs. attest attuned. oregano dash, asplashed. benevolence showers the folk, in lore and in stitutions. a B-heart-minefield. once-neutered bedlam leans into the clusive arms of deckhands. old salt and newer tamarind. a spice of dash. a cool of hand. a puppet of grandiose shuns. there, on the sly

trophied

not + fatten [+ ic]. rough size, bumpy pie. the unwell, impolite cries of 14th-century troupers. personal or senile. twas petual and cidental to notation. abate and reterminate. gold, brass, aluminum, slug paint. be wary, be been. petuity clines unflower to tint, a philosopher's grit. fie!

dicate

from, to. forward, ex go away. or decide. who ate walnut pie. dick? jane
ate him back. hoodwinked lends motorcycle skills to the down-and-over.
be that support and claimant, or tractingly. do take. whyfore take thee?
butter melts into books. do not chew my cake. paper or micro? at last at
least at loans. still: no

duct

toward away. genderings that wander as tucked, as trading. then duck,
then mask, then rewind. too soon, too copious. then phone call. cruciatingly,
this troversy of force cunning, or limb axis, or forensic injury. neither wit,
nor proof of war, nope

hor

more like aversion than frost. bristle away, or have at it, or bore me via
this dearth of jests. countrymen bleed into hoop-skirted bounty. that slip
of the thumb. that besting by wool sleeves. anchor pronto, before you
caustic. now bring on the vivial shudders, the hospitable spines, plus
plenty of anti-

jure

forswear but don't swear. by your minions. by gazoots. a gown and a negate, pudated. all's in, when that one's out. trained jurors doubt. eschew by doubling up the cant. splay forward in vigorating municipal globules. duced

lative

by melting or rejuncture. blatant or cathartic purging. vaporizing via the church, or surrounded by a sports dome. tennis, anyone? syntactical carrying: away, away! or blue-grey marine smears. a late martyr awaits storied ransom. the soccer ball with his foot; in vinyl, too

olish

to grow to destroy. olé and polish and Polish and delish. oy, you want cabbage root with that Indo-European? breviations for the faint-hearted. unauthorized trajectory to a back alley in the one-city province. write-on and dis-permit. whom ditched who? *grow up*

omination

begin during Abbott's Flatland. progress toward an object of. advance several omens. riff off ominable. develop an of. a greatly horred thing, a thinged thing. favourite bogey of his bête noire father. art, or. a baton of monks. fined for loathing learners: as with humankind. a shame, a plague, a trocity

scond

in the south: go south! frequently avoid a left jab to the side of the head, an uppercut to the chin. O Nathema, you rascal! I second that. spurious and spuriouser. take a powder, decamp and skedaddle, famously ebb and wane. occasionally with condiment

sence

to be, or. after the original, after scented pletes. betray the tear ducts, the mauve-dark tunes, the corrugated séance. solve umpteen. but not by the tips. true vision replays the foreplay. that said, where does down point? what time pleads for second place?

solute

free and self-sufficient and true and perfectly. loosen your collar, hitch up those slacks, retie one shoelace. forage amid word-fields, each a straight line, each a straight line. no Mr. In-between in this song; the chorus shouts ahead. maintain no sentential object, blink twice for maybe. solve this puzzle

sorb

clutter notwithstanding. your bent cycle, through and through. nastier than the dictionary. engaged fallout. forsook, and toothsome. commercially ble and dual. clattering as if

stain

from avoiding from. to hold back. taken aback. taken from from. one drop of cherry liqueur on his abjutting chin. strain and stress away. aways away. pull into, keep for keepsakes, evade. more of a stained defrain. frained

stract

the world inside this plastic globe inside this side, in the inner. track my words, mark my toes, lead with the left. sufficiently black tie, but no trace of the suffix. interact and teract. race to straight. or bent. or byways. a thousand times, a hundred, a whole bunch, and then: then

surd

can't carry a tune to rest the mind. definitely not congruous. or finitely
stute. precede with a *the*; from the thinking ear, from the flective hum. no
echo, no jingle, no crunch, no jangle. posterous, ragged, augural bliss. say
no more, no more

undant

wave-waving away. mittens galore and liberal woes. add damn, and damns.
bury rich bundles under lentless water. sleep the nap of the bothersome.
nathema to the blank page; previous painterly lobby; a set-up for the titled.
or less than. whistle with your left tear duct. echo with the right

aptable

too fitted, to modificate, to unequate herence; of being, becoming. sketch out the ac/ad in acclimate, or in adspect. exactly for later – no ipods or ijohns or iprimes. ap, ap, and away! actly – the close-up gathers lilies, the pea pods assemble rhombus husks. pitiable A-frames lean into the Chinook wind. the dairy hives. the blueable strapless. addash, adtribute, adhandedly, damantly

hesive

laminate his followers, caps off! thirteen dentists abjure the lower gums, guns away! away with away, or he'll stitch postage onto heavy-metal aprons. add and subtract 'co-' then deduct tract, but act fast. submissive, substantial, subterranean, get away! now that steel-toed boots stamp pinafores, who's left to lick his squashed buffer? adieu

jacent

germanic yes, as well as our unrude keepsake. the slang glide into overs and tones. adjoin lie to ent. then chortle, but with a hand key. aha koi. rich and richer, piles topple piles. bluebs bejewel me. the exact opposite furthers the winning side. run and runnor. write and writor. neverland blabber

jective

not trippily nor bluely nor hungly nor norly. ventive and ventricle. syntax
swerves via mordant dyes. old-fashioned hat-tipping and ruby-crested
walking sticks and bowing from the knees. throw bones, pitch umlauts,
heave coverlets. after this slanting besure, end on the fine, refine the
defining uptalk

journ

between yesterday and tomorrows. one more Hollywood scene on that
suspension bridge. gaffs so open, the biplane glides right through. buffalo
courts and podiums and car tunes and mustard gavels. place a diurnal
comma, then a comma. legislated journey into joint mythology. half the
bees then the knees. halt Lucifer's interns. groom darlings to mulgate, to
shelve, to divvy the ledge

junct

qualifying but not essentially. or self-luded. several times, several
sectioneds, several tinctures, just not punctuation. circummed toward
verb-hooks. because the tinted service trance open just as the maryjane
mained vulnerable. mal-justed crikey, already! see: *dis-*

mirable

a faucet itself fines luxury. thuh asteroid chips. funny how health scripts
the aforesaid, and then the forementioned. adroit sourcefulness? the gist
plays on. the mirage, the miracle, the mean. sweep past the rabble, mire in
the mortal. ava mural, the 15th century swoops on, laundry pulley and all

monish

scalding lip service vites a dipping sibilance. thus. why dress as a lady
when umbrellas will do? the silver slate slides sideways. can't you just;
don't; be have! toward ad vises! forward-facing hints: meringue underbelly,
fast surfing, warmer bets. lecture against milder squalors. don't be ware
what's ahead

olescent

adnourished. herald and then clare. go back to nourish. herald and then clare. imburse the sultan. wide-brim hats mind to buckle onstage. less as the sun's scent. buoys ply and turn. many a many idol in the backseat. but how many gulls?

ore

not *that* jar! formally, and very highlyly. adumped and adaptionated. send the clowns to uppity school, piss on ants, slip-slide the ads this way and that day. don't reach, but stretch credulity into the mission; admit it. admire ire. asking for dears – but which sister? O the honey of sweet cones! thou yields. play nice, play by the rules, play by ear, play the fields. if ever

ulation

tail-wheedling. plus horsehair. your fondness for vintage DVDs out-wags my lipstick talisman. organic but not always animate. clockwork in the uvula. Canada's poet laureate walks his ferret. smooth taliation for a buck. don't always early; unclearly dulterate those orange yolks

ult

choative dolescence. spective stock in the western world. not a dolt. nor yet dull femurs. supply the left-handed turns. his descending son. front of the frontseat. a chebab and a pachuco don't walk into the bar. but how many gullets?

versity

hostile front facing. calamitous wringer. our curdled nadir. their pumpkin curse. my six-pack sorrow. his festival knuckle. your tributary tinkle. her helmet hand. behold, your clarinet cannoli goalkeeper! even a fool, yes even poets rush in

vertise

good vice for the forlorn. quate this amanting diamond with a likely lance. a lace advocation. a dication toward vanquishing chess piece. why? because waning greens: writer, homeowner, banks. no to foster, to threaten, to touch your toes and then your nose. the public known. the veritable buy-line in Brussels sprout. now puff

auto-

crat

to beeline from mine to yourn. herently correct. pressive, from kingdom. bypass the *amuse-bouche* cravings, oughta matically. his author, despotted. bitty and jointed, dangered by pluttifications. care not who treads or rethreads. booked deals unclaim somnia. promise, don't miss. more candiclandi quatrains at the astrid surkus

mation

formerly the quality of classic ism; animated coining. but seriously. motor and harder, robustly into a saloon. waiver before you estimate. begone, mis-strued clusion! bionically stated twentieth-century fjord. feed the pirate, swallow the lawn gnomes. by hook or by prentice. hand linchpin, handed tropiary

maton

the folded golem, idiomatic of rest or repose. posed thus, we shape and shake. blame omvoluntary thinking, beseech voluntary philosophy. especially those liberations. all he heard was 'train station.' not a bad first pull of whisky to hide side playing cards; play side-'n'-seek. leave structured trivances to those fessionals who speak with an iron-pleated tongue. with or without lingual mastication. flow with the go

nomy

nominal rules, pronominal mayors. always allow the nuns of re and intro. spect no more. yes, you let me. a homicide of kay-o-tees plus a merit of ka-yoots [*see cartoon insert*]. extra, no less. has been granted, all for one. for one. don't pensity, cuz there's room for more brainy gore (or none)

psy

pulsively clinical self-sight. optic demise as post-ex and post-auto, but nary an ante. the con of sciousness, the toe of dropsy. tap water sprinkles onto loose skin, delves into vealed pores, slices through cuts. also figures the extent of changes. likewise: bay at the moon, strike twice for tuitous trans-lations, ever failing this ultimate exam. an unlearning

be-

haviour

verbed possessions. stuffed bears and glossy marbles. always vent before
noon. valor before valour. duct yourself to the cumstance. in a Vancouver
downpour: the National as band, not news. surf wander after electrons, but
in Grade 7, atoms stay put. vie for antibiotical vivisequencing. adhere and
adhold. essay clingwards and daze juggling. sequinsing genes, behemming

hest

more promise than command. bespeak the knack. ever more. as in: behight,
no rogue. extra turmeric and repeat the quest. befriendly treaty, unsuss the
pre-colonial, boxed on all sidles, like a blue-blood test. ungrudged an English
daisy or locomotion carrot. select a language, betake a number, please

holden

way past the vective finishing lineation / I'm telling ya! benign holdings.
belated cigars and chessboard burrows. caw such as gratitude, field more
in the credit card family. what doesn't rhyme with moral aspect. does
rhyme with bebolden deprived of its suff[ ]. just give me a minute to free
that mockingbird

queath

utter and quoth, via at on to or for. just barely bi. your query my quest?
beneath but not underqueath. can deliver any melon bequired, really. one
quince and a handful of quinoa, legally bespoken. when my breath seizes,
every disposable will see or hear that buzzing fly. smirch that dash of
poetry, behalved to you. the exhaled word

reaved

particled snatch and plunder. smears former loved ones, then latter environs.
be valid. done to, yet spirit of your deity. define as: lated bejoicing. much
leaguered. a right angle and a left triangle. bespoiling for a match does
taminate the waning. a dollop and a torrent. yesterday's full moon blends
fever with today's orphans. today's peppermint deluge. reft, even

seech

stop with, then gerrymander. a beetle, a leech, an ick. two winds from the
north. some seechers seechingly scuttle. but why? how is not the time. I'm
certain to questingly marry. deny the odds, play the rhythm & blues. saxo-
phone, with an accent. besought to behinder, but not beseemly. sermons
and Shakespeare: rummaged brethren, just a pint-sized dragon. speech
eech to beep

sotted

to stupefy with drink [in/ex: love]. past tense but not before. ginger root
then grapes then mango pulp then eluctable peels. on the ground or hang-
ing, the joke's bounded. guiled and fatuated at the first espy. my heart beats
sotto voce, in tandem and tentionally. how's that for a California tangerine?
the paragraph break tosses me aside. the sides of the photo melt inwards.
tween and twixt betrothings. witched. each billet-doux an acouplet, esp
with his be-blotted eyes. think: bloodshotted

ware

when cargo freightens pro-duct, before. my last article was an *an.* ware the bespeckled. under, not over. ear to the ground; lips to the page. his wary defence leaps off the sheaf onto my hyoid. my hands. my 4-D ear canal. garage sales in the basement. not if you don't like spicy. unperative caution yields Whistler widow hawking wild plums at a BCE crossroads. mighten and mangle. are too, dos. where? always under

bi-

ennial
maybe lasting, maybe occurring. with a pear leaf blister of distilled raspberry juice. bye bi a dolescent. fixed ends, radical Zs, and unaccented foreheads. any alphabet implicates the lobster bisque, the goat bistro, the gusted ennui. fun yet?

furcate
two forks, this time. as in Y-styled flowers, not XY. try a morsel of smidgen, don't binge! I'd cater to mammals, but bison flick the apex. or snake vertebrae. select a language, then splurge. dulge. gorge. how Xmas of you. how mag. how cone-bearing. nuff

gamy
tripod passion. venison shames mutton chops, fronts sarcastic seafood. a certain tripolar condition leads to diehard hypocrites. connect the geometry at the edge of your face, Geo to his (half-life) friends. the hermit decides to gape. yawn and quish. then pluck

nocular

eyefold card deck. often practised in the plural. who's to say the impassive voice ain't what it used to be? fitted prisms reword eccentric rectangles. nocturnal lairs and nautical radio waves. those biggest bigots sometimes beard the search-engine stubble. another bling rivalry amends each tee-totaler. bionically

ped

or thick. birds or human births, diagonally. better to vote bipartisan or bilabial. prosaic and humdrum. 'slong as you amble on that bicycle. quite the manly bionic bimbo. a million + a million, counting Batman. her biz may brace voluntary fauna, or itchy sons. this doppelgänger opts for more altruistic zoology. foreplay will be foreplay. byblos scrolls: right as my right leg

agulate

miscuously, at best. a gent of alescence. often even as co-co. the kiss between milk and lemon. co-necked, then co-noodle. surround my heart like a byzantine crown; roguish bawd, in the bod, like an unDracula-dagger. jelly, egg white, clotted soup, conut oil in January. all that is buoyant melts into the 19th century still not a party

alition

and with teenagers. twice the dex, now deeply matose, flips past the cohesitation to legislated grammar, along with military formations. that prehensive late Latin that bites one in the Aloysius. regards to your tonsils, bouncers of the backdrop foyer. sweat and then climb. tons more quisite cargo. cluding feminist lions, but only ablatively

erce

to timidate and to pel. when closed, arks force the quiry, duce the primer, gest the summary. enfierce the diatribe, the trovertible brogue: my own, not yet unproper

gitate

deeply. chewing, and a sidering. a bildungs wander, a blast from the past, *gesundheit!* terminal covetousness. anyone in need of Hollywood-style gnitive calibration? wallow in the mud. hair of the dogless. gestate toward the open ward, gravitate hoveringly. a gate and a total abmission

herent

in as well as ad or here. certainly smearing rutabaga henna. us, us, us. when smoking is thinking, Hannah Arendt films herself. father's ginger root pacemaker presents a ruthless wherewithal, but with *some* ado. T or F: high-heeled runners or this vernacular neck brace

hesion

trinsically brook figurative stammers. and literally. hedonist glue for the ambient human. duo rococo, man! plant parts and organ fallout. rehensible, I dare say. dare ya, but later. if only the onyx called the spelunker bad. we cling to the intermolecular. we fling; we hinge

ital

'the physical vergence of female and male genitalia escorted by rhythmic travels – need valuate against ORGASM.' prate on, truly. frequently, Italian. italics list ligatory liqueness. photo may be a porcupine inside a python. he is quietus, she is multi-culti. say it with me: go coit yerself. 'six of my favourite terms.' welding. skip the next word in the cyclopædia (you don't need me to terrupt). by the mutated shores: 'once a planetary force.' yep. to go and fare thee well

com-

batant

with one, such as a person. blatantly without the edians or padres. batively paring: bative, bative, bative. pugilistically peting. tofu burgers smothered in ontology, if fortably partmentalized. don't sneeze on my toes. don't breezy. a worm may pel the apple gainst your lips. or again. heralding bat boots. sometimes roosters

bination

two × two. rely on petent echo sequencing. an act or state or dumpling. how bustible your figure! how partible! one union of separations quals the sorry goose. every morning, croissants with binary butter. together gether. mutations and draughts. shall we lip-glide? a prickle of hedgehogs. a chord of underwear. plex and bo, we worry together. then gether. found and pound: for the nation. pulsory serviettes with your deckchairs, all hands

pany

with an 18th-century panion. or 13th-century bread with lemon hodgepodge. a strict admixture of soldiers. plural of mole. glimpse what she spoke, her ponytail q-marked and k-ed. who we're having, who we're joying. who's acting pansy. broadcasting and dot(com) and diculous pipelines and eggshell knights. don't forget to bolden the firefighters. or to part: 2s

pensate

floors and tops, weighted spinning. balance the plus sign with the equal signature. her Grade 10 reckoning. soft alchemy. you owe me, buddy. *his over- [verb] for his un-*. one cell for the next, one bean for the many, one further. recoup

placent

self-gratify, but without the thrills. more suns, more noses, more Connecticuts. to a fault, but not to two. ripe pear. sour triplets. don't go varying... such a lukewarm fever flames the bright bulb of environmentally commended light fixtures. methinks certain zombies wobble plicitly, but without the kill. untheist

plement

to not plain, to tensify. withered pea shoots flatter the soup. the pliance may be mine, but all pliments originate with you. routine blood plasma, s'long as we pose 90° from wedding vows and nautical grammar. stir in one pliant pimento; a cascade of beta-blockers. add: supple mints. add: tincture and variant spelunk plunderings. he's handsome all right, fold from the corkage

ponent

chemical sure locks. beware a knot of toads. pwned and pwned again. founded posites, that's why. or founded rumours, that's *not* why. oily punctions. net yield's prehensible. if at times you taste a soupçon of versary challengers, turn over. the orange-juice add-on. penting his chin nod. key pancreas: 'he my dad'

pulsion

as much as punction. as Freud in Lisboa: *obrigado!* exactly imaginable, like sequential bow ties. whereas ankle cuffs suggest a quiver of cobras; suggest a prompt rodeo buckle; the past tense of lentils. unsay dialectical squeeze-play. urge. voke. suade. throbbing qualms for one's shame-limb

pute

to prune or pave. prone to astute mutations. multiply a thousand by days, then craftily assuage the pudenda before birthrooting this dragonfruit. thank youx. first arouse the taunting breadbox, or overlook the descript catsuit. youx welcome. to grasp Galician, you must hand over every hang-over. reckon so

rade

handsome is as stubble does. a scurry of squirrels as comroguery. such a long way from chamber-shy. hip-hip for the radical commode – not *that* kind of party. always fraternal, nary a consort. better hob-nob in sleep, better crony than cohort. chortle, man

con-

[for more sults, see 'pro']

clusive
leading to no def or re. three clues under the hope chest in the false attic.
she knows. the left breast or the right, nestled into the lining or the cervix.
solutely: tirely and tally. more than a booster shot, more than visits to the
mall (seventeen). more than the usual con. en-dash-cluding siding along.
heed west

cur
less than he might

quer
more than he should

viction
culpable and suasive and truthed. 'opinions for kids.' kid-kids. kick-
starting the ground, from the vulsions to the date-dates. vincing and demn-
ing, or just plain ane. this plate over this borrowed leather pouch; this
person over several binders. the one true luckette over every doomed else

vince

vinny, and a revved-up handcart – go! you don't need to buy my hat to toss it into the shattered ring. being entirely fathomable. just not giving an inch. prisoned by creed. utterly and clusively. look up, bend down. now only fabulate

bauchery

to make them abhor you, but in a frolicking way! down, off, away, among.
then utterly undo. how to debunkum parliament. we all can't celerate, it's
full zip a head. licious, lirious, lectables – must I spell cadent out? or may
I hex testable scura?

bilitate

away from potency, but in a gendered way! he liberately molished the
check mark, right up until his bonair manner bated my breath. had me in
that bulldog choke: 'a reverse guillotine, if you like.' gosh and sternation,
eh? I'm feebing out, man; I'm stroking in, femaled entity

famatory

ruined tittle-tattle, a nial for a corative river. mine that calamity janet, but
leave plenty of room for off-duty forestation. draw the puppy or the
football, eh? chase more odorant. add a comment, here. vour me. he's such
a little vil, if only by monic possession. tenure for the mons

fect

therapeutic carnivals. fickle and goaty. form facetiously, that'll learn 'em. de-sadism for the amateur sperado. fiance and person and body part, in that confusement. to disown or to blemish, take your elite pick. one's the best choice, the choiciest percentage. tox and ter. claratives for the extra sleepy

fiant

unfaith me. bold mutiny for the gimpy ear. a gasp and then an under. they legate, right up until Relenting McPlorable becaptivated them. but he meant ficiently, eh? (always tach from the exclam!) cline fewer pyramids, fibrilate further privations. the lone mands the hungry; the hungry don't eat

formity

good body, bad body. good mentia, bad lusions. we three monarchs feed you a tatorship. R U in? the extra toes and the antler, the hair and the funct. Mr. Mister woos nobody. since and after. then before again. wheels brake for other wheels. further to our signation, that ficiency sucks

mocracy

in theory. each cathlon sprints across cartography, but with colourful contours, 'cay? love how you molish the pop. love the mographics. love how you marcate all terment. to wit: love the vout votion. all finitions translate from page to air, from hand to posse token. dilettante this

monstrate

the ongoing public divine show. unlook Miss Creation. while one handfest shows ception, the other increases by nought cibels. so why muster? to flaunt a steinian hemoth. to later operate, but as feelings. understated gloom-light and a muted wish-light

nigrate

to blacken; circa 1526
fang the dusk, gulp through surgency straws
wheretofore apples? frying pans? manifold snakes in the wheat?
he gulfed and gulfed they
festoon and lusional, he lounged where he never longed. I crumble finity snow
I showing not telling. dude, be grateful. dude, be not meagre nor miserable nor ple
no spoken ctators, here or there or biquitously. only a slip
on the tongue rooves
only ever stakes

nouement

avec accent aigu. literary roller coaster with a one-way trip to Mars unleashes the
post–*not yet.* ravelling carefree, peanut arcade letions. first, we give you pie
charts, then we tie one *at.* busy-busy, like a dangered bee in your *ya-ya* fedora.
é? what up? both lovers: in the coda

pravity

as in: stinancy, unwanton bauchery, and irrighteous ultation. more than emptory
in this 'verse and maybe others. the city bus cons the freeway taxi. remember to
floss. quality or state, I bet my purse on his manly rouge. scond a little kink in the
benevolence. erroneous-headed, she joked about his thingamabob. first-known
cholera was a snip-tempered harmonica. period

precating

first oil and gas, and now selfies preciate all day long. deke and deny and deft,
then debtingly sent from. pray away, but in a defatigable way. avert that kind
of trash talk. cipher a word; ject the wonder. plenty velopment in the valley.
fully 78 percent of the Usage Panel this week

reliction

tirely linguished. as a noun, and at sea. of piss-pants and of duty. seventy-one tusks lost in one day. and your mitts. international failure and one-leaf clovers. if only you meant this in a ds-bolic way. I'm ds-gnosed and I'm vastated. yellow beats taste as fragsome. born on every day saps and unhands them. can you cern the colour of my birth eyes?

rision

and at sea world. exactly the same as translution, but with a down-laugh. more mock than jeer. more target than wimp. or limp. supplementary sentences from Genesis. lyrical on-the-rise. because he serenades female you. pshaw, pshaw. and in Psalms, too. even God partakes, then ticipates. then packs up the ol' kit bag

spicable

you. worthy of voking them to craft the vile. and parade her merit. tender tune for the juice harp. scope on the down-low. pict this paltry organ and the trophy will cide luck or doom. vroom-vroom. we know these words

sultory

should you really flate his span-new solation? he's licate and spairing, doncha know. but in a vantaged way. tell all your friends, then your mom. this vocabulary ends in the middle. nope, doesn't. soul spatch oops guards. some evenings sag from the downpour up, but in a function-key way! spoiler alert: anyhoo

teriorate

second-rate stem. prisons and your health and the nation's highways. less corum about terror and a bit of rivation, yes? tective meets time-travelling decursor. your meanour says it all. go to pot, go to the dogs, go to ancient Greek bris and mains. just don't go to sleep. first the mirror kiss, then the post-breakup half-hearted sulk, then the anthill riots. I mean that in a totally scriptive way!

viant

clearly, other people. to siccate organic tritus, rub in a trimental ways-away. don't ceive yourself, your kernel of tegrity lives on. like before, but viva, eh? he's linquent about soluteness, but dead-straight about the luxe sounding board, the bondage suite. wowza

abled

      'pensible; here, merely pejorative'

aster

star-crossed calamity

an asterisk for the astrologically challenged

de-bolden debacles

      downgrade the recurring crucible

an if

    an expectorant

        pects for the imflawed future

don't trek inside, but grade on a curve – embowel the thesaurus, creetly

    wowsa?

combobulated

dis-open the stanza, half-witty and enfranchised
      whimsical decomposing
         even the experts probe cretionary hand-holding
who'll measure those sheets in perfect array?
      his heartening dain for the oriented
        pluck another piano wire from the cordant web
           plenty of cool knick-knacks to hail

                                          gruntled

and viaduct groans, and gruntles, grumbling
turtles clench the adjective's nest, a participle or a particle
just nother ad- or dis- or ab- or con-
how sitting the sour un-
excellent, how a shoe-horse may tumble, collapse
on your knees, on your belly, on your bare-evicted abs
now: sway to the thymed rhymes

gusted

to trigger tasteless. in someone else
the 'ed' bestows the bad, underlines with red pen, tries for a thumb sideways
fed to the top teeth: too much to eat rivals sick, rivals ds-ease
smacks of tinctive loathing
disforms. a mal and a miss
whenever you slant, they uncard, they decreate
        they past-participle the hevelled junction
    hey-hey-hey, don't bingi-bongi!
each banana peel too concerted to ambiguate the 'Take 2'

parage

the figurement
the ciplinary reaction or the crawl-space posal
the parate pairs and the uneasy husbandry sertations
    the silent sident slides to partake in the ample tumbleweed
hearken February turbances
bleed the challenging sonance from the participled verb
then sipate the corporate kiss-off – BAM!

rupt

to rot tomatoes stemming from cerning taste, criminating beets, yet
the downtown bus plays the claimer:
    cover and covery
you might want to arm yourself by cussing every savoury character
    gag and gaga / gage and guise – vent steam or especially sudden
        'popcorn popping on the apricot tree'
  our ranged hymns travel at prosthetic-neck speed
off rumps
dify in unpreparation
 ¡ándale! ¡ándale!   &   *dale vs. hill*
one before the plosion: earth sciences and vulva volcanos
    don't diss the v-word, glaze mountains of lations, each stroke to the left
    each paddle to the midriff
        up and up, veers blue and bluer
    turquoise cross-stitching, and abandon the Andes
    and these
             : full ds-
               closure

traught

                there's no puting winter tress

come early, stay late   #too taught, too troubadour

               no disgenuous pology necessary

seminate the seminal, trust the tinguishing feature, misgive the ds-doubt

        keep your tance: we flaunt our tomas

                        to finite traction. now: *PERSE*

turb

        to untrust

to gorge and gorge again

dis-march, then dis-april

pel the thought

swipe card for free – no strings! – wins

he's sooo picable, am I right or am I left-handed?

communicate your sense echo, portionately yours

every time, they tell us to get used to a quieting verdict, a quieter dict _e-_

gregious

tinguishable herds and flocks. ceptional (cept now) dread, right? am I ripe or am I rotten? minently reregarded, roar ffeminate rror, or spicuously low-drooping pears, pending on ironical cattle. prior to exit and sequent to ego trip. gariously social. versed!

ject

out of but not quite x, that breviated lectra. without the rechargeable sparkling hands. turfed comic books, 3-D cartoons, and kids' movies for grown-ups. mock-Cyclops for the computerly challenged. bachelor taxes for ovulating property. c'mon, don't be that ousted database

rect

and rection. mergency up: lineations from the 1590s. try mayonnaise with your e-like mathematics, while numerating. sprinkle some physics onto that flagpole. awake or archaic, plish or plash? or: exalted with blood. statues and gerbera stems and crossword puzzles and pricks and pendicular guidelines. lofty and swollen, jus' sayin'

vade

the lastic of your credit card delibly scrapes my skin. a minion and a mouse. a sly maze and a house. the dexterous con of pelling critters. no blueberry quation minus some lusive lixir. be sure to break naan bread, only aseated in egalitarian gondolas. not vasive, nor ventual. quivocate the qual and the quibbles. outskirted and defoxed: see vamoose

viscerate

the quivalent to bowel. gut the vertical locutions, fillet the longated nunci-ation. gorged guava. one eye or two secrets. practice a cumvention, just don't junct a darker jade. bullient Channel 4 ratings. enough

volve

if only. so unDarwinian, between Duchamp's preferred staircase and the rolling pletive. vacuate biology and vict the fish. quite the laborate way of tracing nectarine blossoms and sniffing beagle sketches. par chances to metamorphose. 'I'm Samsa!' yeah? educe this

bargo

calm the nation stampede. port the merchants, hibit the ships. no use barring any foul language: aaarrgggh or bastardo or gopher. lete a photo veto or one caramel-candy no-no. gulp. go-go lads may suggest a tolerant taboo. I have one caveat: neon icicle bottleneck

barrass

to plement plexity. ply blue-letter bibles and an obvious pun. pede or fluster. abashed in the basket or flurry in the silo. *please*. the more populated bus-stop menades and phone-booth hampers or hinders. stet

bellish

to nearly cause to render as ornament, to bewreathe. bed Bob Edwards into riverside property and your firm bankment goes belly up. the armadillo burped daintily into a porcelain glove. just as sixteen rabbis voted for baroque church glockenspiels. or bellish fingers curled backward until left elbow left. crease that aggeration. dish

bezzle

leather jacket and a striped sailor kerchief. mind me to gouge. or sneak dizzy into dification. muddied pilfering, on the bedazzled side. emerald earring dangles from extended lobe. bro, don't sleep through property taxes. how to embetter yourself in Nepali: dispense long vowels and unspirated plosives

blem

the opposite of bling, a bossed replicate. ballistically speaking, we shall recite the dictum or motto, boldened. so to recap: en+bold+en. heraldic blahs feed the rhinoceros and the eagle. balmed mosaic devil stamps blend our no comment. read and weep. blazed and broiled, minus the bodied hornbook

broider

purl the dainty armadillo. proto-germanic pro-braids, minus hornbooks. followed by upon. 'he faggoted the blouse for his wife.' no pun. less an bryonic hero than a pired pathos. oh yeah? stitch that vest bristle before roiling ooze emanates from the crewel-side. once, then once

ployee

plies the ee, then makes use of the creases, the tangles, the votions. O hail initiator and criminator: be volved, be plicated, at least for minimal pensation. one peeled Kartoffel, and eleven swallows. not zoiks, but hint harder. a single dewdrop below the cutive. I'll sider a gandy-dancer over a temp, a toiler over a flunky. *eek!* but what does an emu emote?

en-

amoured

to typically Aunt Amy. more or less caustic; more or less encephalitic.
thralled by, chanted by, witched by. tranced by all those voiced liquids.
flamed by fessional poetry. sotted by half-and-half. usually with with.
ephemerally fatuate

croach

inhooked, or pass wrongfully. rightfully. fullfully. the obvious catatonic
roach-clip slipping skinny-dips into wayward mouths. oh for a mouthful-
fully. culpate onto the football field, onto posturing grassland, onto a neigh-
bour's desert inroads [esp. stealthily]. purl one, crochet two. the worm and
the stagecoach. encrustedly

dearment

such as affection, two dollops of. or more verisimilitude alongside
marmosets, poppets. the fatherless encircle the higher estimate. but glom
onto de cariño to ensure catcalls. she was always deglamorized. a first
inside thirds. my skies! my eyes! the ABBA to any kiss! how many curtains?
get ripped

deavour

multiple marsupial courts flounder then flonder. don't put yourself in owement, own the choosement. three divas short of a punctuation choir: exclam! have you had mincemeat for breakfast? do you do inorgasmic truffles for keeps? an adage, an age, this page. this many bent hoops? prefer the bendable loop. devoid and desist, only not until NumLk. syllable!

dure

not gladly, and no gadflies flit overtly. make solid, make duress. over 437 caterpillars, under seventeen moths. silk screens, but no no-see-ums. practical give-way. erstwhile roundabout. two livers, four kidneys. again. two lives, four kids. not again. review the debotched material. dust your gloves. suffer the negade hardening. all unto

ergy

a simile for Aristotle's vigour. ergetic and ergeticer. one spurt of that breakfast grapefruit, two ternal bustion pulses. measure in joules, in jouissance, in fantasy jousts. work that spiritual adrenaline – one more, one more, one more! blazing with ch'i, ch'i, ch'i, ch'i-vibrations. by means of that organ which is more than wrought, it's

hance

gorged lipstick and happy aspirin. haughty fences and pursed hip-hop. exalted kitsch and fattened triceps. nose augment and nosey spatter. case study and sturdy casings. ha! and haw-haw. called-for trigger and magnifying-glass sparks. retouched snaps and touchy crowns. baked habits and utensiled cakes. tannin and mould. or (bellish)

jambment

engorgeous torque. me 'n' hambone flect pennies for the fella. straddle the pro-mavens, boys, Stein's a-coming! stride from lyric enclave to prose engine. yes. recite with peachy jam and cured hog. forget the cure, best treatment: rupture, cessate, vivify. unpause the couplet at every semi-climax. mend, then acerbate

mity

to not at all Aunt Amy. a standing nervation a bit exnervating, a tad unnunciated. from that loutish chestnut, we mighty re-fab. a very deep unfriendly. exactly that. so how to ex-umerate their wage? how to capsulate latent almonds? revulge the cumbrance. spise the hoary nuisance. her sneeze heaven-sent. in vulnerable I trust

ormous

off-side; norms so meant to be broken (cept this one). starboard-rules-foosball! steal the quay to my heart. less entity, more icon. as in, grammatically wicked. *he's* titled but *they're* the emy? originally, aye. mayhap stipulates invious intrapment. forward splurge. I'm elated to end at invy

sconce

the dearth of scones. moonwalk repealed by Pre-Raphaelite earthwork. might I con thee? might we bundle the kindling? settle this sentence: argue for snug. haitch before aye-aye. overwrought bivouac. too soon, too smug, too parade-y. mere minutes to tablish and to cape. then before when

thuse

to rhapsodize, to eager, to exhil. gradually, over time (not yet, not yet). idle news. neighbourly chartreuse. thus spake disputed scholarship. in god he thrusts. pre-dating entity and post-courting enrapturous. semble the sembles. be ecstasied. while we pay heed, she encunts you

velop

perhaps Celtic. don't hate on entropy when you can amend those irksome enzymes. my visage microbes your dorsement. our finale unmasks the paper snapdragon, flip to: cantas OR antes, chilada OR almanac. quicks OR quires: unwrap up the reveal

equi-

librium

uniform scales. or books floating in the basement. the sum of all zero torques. but fewer ponies. pay 25¢ and ride in one direction only. plumes and plumes of mental floss. the p of nox. of the ne valency (of valley). have I mentioned the thermal corset patent? have I?

vocate

when you interpolate a matching tag. at this end: hogs and gators; by the sidestep: fudge and waffles. circumvention for kids. before varicating, we dither in the dahlias. rhymes with alias. you're ternally it

ex-

[in with the 'outs']

for-

lorn

to prompt the miserable wretch, hoard the past participle of praved. to be deity for saken. to bandon all former nications. to go and to originate. *is that right?* to accurately spurt apple pips. to bargain a dreary release that refunds that lugubrious sky hook. too triste in the east. to author the mud on the dais in the linguistic circus. to gloom. O lorne

becile
the opposite of a stick: 'above an idiot and beneath a moron.' some tasks, under, super vision. for the best and foregone, for the west and woebegone. not a desmirching yet belligerent. not a prat but a tosser, not a schmuck but a numbskull. beneath a dumbskull and above a dumbhead. but not a deadhead? corporeal, before 1802. agine that, if

broglio
in a boil. and then [verb]ed: bued, pacted, paled. so many more maculate inklings than dandelion tea in a Saskatchewan blizzard. stir the pot, but don't push it in the envelope. a 1750 heap of torn boughs; a messy 1819 novel. impeach the apricot alfresco passe. personate no one

minently
mediate migration; to jut upon dwelling. bricate the mons glans. gather and loom, noun and etc. 'cold showers are awesome.' infused by the roots, by the lexicon. immediate imagery, imagism, magi bathrobes. a tegrally greedy mansion, with a dash of perialism. wave at the flag parade. seek: one heat-suffused popcorn kernel

molate

bibe this passioned plea. coffins built from calamity and sulphur. a sprinkling of spicy disciple, the previous meal boasts salsa and crow and Alice/Wilma kissers. two glasses of dandelion wine, generous portions of barley cake, and one overpriced gallon of scapegoat. you and Aztec and Troy and [S]elf ... and forever us

munity

begin at im-impair. itate how textbook hornets personate mix foragers and partial platforms. lementary theatre prov. to resist, to ject, to acquire pulsive legumes, repel each artificial volcano. harried sorrow – oft granted through a Sumerian beer straw

pede

or don't. gotta love those backformations, oh-so-penetrable, and oh-so-vasive. his wooden nickel in a penny jar. his yoked pecker in a scene-stealing beehive. ensnare the feet, lasso the line / break. bookmark the toe-jam. only measure across his spinal mask, just

pervious

poverished mulling. flinchingly serk and serker. half a watermelon wedgie, with crayoned and quartered seeds. but how do you grow onion rings? tried and tested ne'er-do-ill, but oh-so ponderable, agreed? more petuous than rash, more phlegm than plement, more tinent than prank. freeze halfway to Zeno. orcize each jaywalking spree, press on a pish neck tattoo, and guzzle prisoned doubloons. and then formerly. every memo a wildered perative

petus

petting safari, us vs. sign the petition! thirteen ways to stanza the deadline. more with a feather. how to portune pressionable railway labour: precate, I swear. don't give me that line, document on the dotted catalyst. paper and panions. sign in, sign away, sign down. the poem must marry the pimento

placable

placebo, for reals! place ogre on the front dash, centred. every capable cable shadows the ceiling plug-in. fret, then print the 19th-century button. again with verbial arch emy. unpliant and uncaving. rubicund hoodoos cringe with basalt dust, even when painted onto the Turkish lira. don't go, don't be a stranger, don't chase fairy waterfalls. break throbbing chimney hearts

plicit

upon touch but not trusting. unvocal folding. urban anger over chamomile math – liken $xy + x^2$ to $y^2 = 0$. pay attention, this is portant! hint at this faux-leather tailoring. inexplicated 'for the rest of your life.' bourbon, or any grained swill. at the very least prefixed by 'al' – then liminate every gebra

punity

xempted penalty. puny rashness. who dunked the punks face first? my Syria, I plore you: do not plicate or pinge! the hurricane munity arrives from the east, then pudently assigns Sigh Language: hard-of-hearing doesn't nearly cover the def. puntastic, do not heed the sequences. dissertation unity thralls idle hands. more *im* than im; more thud than throb. clasp ins & outs

(spired

pired)

-it stage left

ponential posture leads
(out-there) to here

dulge me
eh

how to habit one more clinic for curables
wind about the adequacy of going
cognito. ahem

stigate (again and again) any volution
that luges and lutes, that bites, chews, wraps around
as festations flects to the left
transigent telligensia: add a twirl, toe another footnote

she vertently paged through the bingo vincibles

or the 'verse (, ya know?)

he's ept and epter
to dustrial degrees (*no blague*)
as a baroque aside, they acted ordinately
proud of his ferior novations

who at this quisition deems non-stop sults as sufferable?
yes please

I trapolate nothing; I punge
the entire panded galaxy

when to foliate, when to pedite each
pre-laughable-package

troverts frequently hale
through the other nostril

surmountable?

capacitated?

evitable?

tinct quenching ten times as many
succinctly
a lie pinches the bulbous ink
relate my gait to Australia's tinctions
færies and dodos and Guam's flying fox and a politicized Big Bird
solutely sisting
but finitely not solutely anythinging

( ) order to vigorate the vestigation
sert finger into digital ternet
surgents swell, terpretations abound
stop [.] this stant [,] one of these days I'll veigle some prompt sputum[:]
ceiling swirls stigate bedroom brawls
bedsheets timate and sidious and toxicating!

I'm not sinuating, I'm satiable (real iteration fruit)
flict flict

bleeding the vanilla valise
sanguinate the posed odus

devil fatuation may lead to joyless Halloween parties
carcerated at the front door (shut it!)
clude the Burbank tapings, and I'll sell you more demnity
than can fill your candy bag
onesie cunabula

oculate countering the multiplied eyebuds

seminate 'the cement poem'

what sipid ambling alphabets
pony stagram for the less sured
brick by brick, every frastructure pays for himself
you fidel. you solent ego

flate eleven balloons after midnight. the cumbent always wins:
bamboo against the English

      sung to the meld of orable banking
      uh-huh, the candelabra's plicable blue tremis
      wait, don't wander (save for haustible times)

his mood so resistable (so consolable)
the credulous cubicle lying, incorously
why shred radish seeds? why deniably vey the effable?

furiating, no?
freakingcredible, right?

does flammable count when you tervent?

                ex-right,

57

in my perience

men ploit clusively from the left-handed column queues

corrigible to the (last)
    hibition

who vites you to undate that choir-master,
with whom my manent dignation knows no blunt
struments? cheque please!

do not aggerate your pectorate skills
do not empt or haust yourself
do not hume
the body, you'll only asperate the uberant twins
you'll only plode the radical rungs
do not cuse your (Franklin record tour) pedition
do not exmasculate merging planations
you'll tract fourteen sales on the New Zealand dollar
you'll periment on the unwilling snacks
you'll cite the quisite masses

you'll hort and hort some more
do not pect (pat-your-back) raves
do not plore

Dickinson would argue for the tenuating (*slant*)

coriate rhymes with breviate and bicarbonate (but not carbonate?) in a four-way
corrugated metal spreads itself thin, then thinly, then thiniest
not the extra nasals in tinny (but) a corridor of skin abrasion
could be brassy, could ternalize razor-thick lesions
at first, the asterisk consumes the X, but then the viaduct streams to the core
B4 (under)

the cessant cantation ear-blossoms across
which northern Trans-Canada (only three interchanges)
no literation tended (the ever-trepid terrobang)

alienable rights filtrate waxed ertia

gest this
added gredients grained, but only in the past

does flame measure up when pired?

participle after participle

the scrutable tegrations blanked me on the forehead
true panda-patch flection
true blog
fectious yokes voke nineteen blokes. dubitably

always more trances than ways-a-ways-out

inter-

lude

repeat
       after an oblong peat

ludic   lutes   slink-in to epilogic
                  lyres
       on the down-wave, you'll perceive
                        few involuntary fugues, here
          a frain ceived fectly
          via
          short
          ruptions
a harmed
                   post-amble
      with orange-rind duction and
                       hints of
ludicrous play
                surd and zarre
                      when, now?

[click here to view full lustration]

mis-

cegenation

irregular n. circa 1864
'until there be no antonymity.' O you mixen!
whose trial is it now? cede that to the figuratively ornament
again: inter male and female. improve your gin rummy!
lead and led, follow and suit, mozzie-time and break & shake
et tu, et tu

cellaneous

a mixed bag. definitely mixed-up mobile gnizance. remember that fifties
mixer? shapen meet-and-greet for treated misers. duck out, before your hole
boss steers some chronistic mistletoe. each and sundry: anagram; anapest; O
Annabelle. beware milk deliveries and Tongue Fairies. heed garb-ups and
faddy liveries. don't miss the late-night flicks – midnight's a doozer

chievous

not ogyny. not carried, not coded. neither anthrope nor a bevy of guided
givings. deadpan punchline, hit hard. fun's fun, until the charming get
minor demeanours. rank this list: follow twitter right up until the police
report. filed, again and again, we're drained by the tinual use, by the
handling, by the ever-stabbing. likewise, I'm sure

hap

to feed joy. swallow. a double, then a triple. promptu lawyers heed the itemized. acting. even so, beware the fortunate accident, that railment of a miss. compass the jar of garlic gherkin; cool as a fit forecast

nomer

who nominates whim? he trusts his tresses, palpably. leaves off the mystery pablum and ho-hum lips. more miss than swing. cuff this bat. cuff them swingers. albeit cannot troduce pendents. missy orgies ticipate muffed vocabulary. wrongly waivered, they twist and turn, twist and turn, twist

takenly

at least one jersey jective, at least three taut tentions. calm missile for the lewd anthropic. usually the Windsor International Airport. dingy things: a burst of panther behind bars, those ripening fruit eyelids, a pastel-faded carousel. 'sup?

non-

chalant
definitely no chalice, but lean onto the prefix: 'gnaw' and then 'sha' and then 'lnaw' – Canadian nunciations that flip the fowl, from the plot line to the grassed oh-so-descript horizon

e
imaginary being, such as a harpy or a walrus. first, merge 'i' with 'sp' and 'sc,' then chill. not any nor one. a three-shaped finale. much ado about nonny nonny, hey! and stutter mufflers: la-la, lalage, and lalalla. monosyllabic nonliteration. non-stick pans. nobody twinkle

plussed
not exactly unperturbed, and not more watered. just a bit sprinkled. no spares, only a sprain or two wrinkles. not pissed or livid or living furious, but a dash of plexed. this here's an abacus. only partake in fruit loops for supper. granola for date night: plus one. he, too, wraithfully desists a lot. or a little. yes. sometimes maybe. not nevertheless

sequitur

non-legitimate, yet it does follow ... quitters never success and achievers don't landslide. just the Crowsnest you missed looking for. how dictable, how ginary. as one stops, so one fictions. white collar. blink, blink. here to reference the existent allus: *allus*

ob-

durate

proto-Indo-Euro hardening. or indurate. more like a pathological sinner, moved to scratch below the sternum. how the crotchety young tory loves durable clusiveness. we cavate from the top down, to preserve the sonification. to jelly the egesis to the candescent, but cussed and flinty. guys, eh?

fuscate

as the night unclears, so too does 'Asperger syndrome unclouden.' to befog and bemuddy. I aim to fess up, eat the cake, bury the hefty cheque and check for onscreen navy highlights. O my. fuss and scat! gone fission and fused marrow, slurped through a crazy straw. twice. luminate the guise, the genuous clarations, the biguous. in tend antsies. plastic hope

ituary

phat emplifies what plomats call jectionable jectification. from the dusty crypt where they meet their own reavement, cured words stall. sewn into edient beads then counted backwards. a genre for pituitary peas that annul tiguous rewards. raise dust, raise hell, raise the promenading dead. tuse and tuser, and then some

sequious

fawns and harts and sequined venison. toward following and plying the polka-dotted conforum. veins and knuckles queue for orbit, then seek pliant prudes. then docile questions. then the bendables. then sidian Romans in Ethiopia. all good boys

sess

frequently to besiege-from. vious cover story that leaks lizard droppings and daffodils and flip-page romance. seapaging; seapagination. fusing and fused – for 3426.7 days (+) hours. millificent. an ooze of a whisper. defy sitting, trary to abnormal tensity. there's a banana in your pocket, for sure. re-release me. reefer corrective. in a pickle jar, not barrel

solete

from vious to solete in one claymation minute. able and ation, but only the finest mine fervour. tensify your soul, bleep your sonality. then blanket outward cation to the breeze. whilst this accent vives, mayor rhymes with major, as in: liquely. a tegral piece to the tangent puzzle. olé

stacle

they fight, they don't put any makeup on the face of Replaka. they uproot, they don't steadfast soldier. they rehitch, they don't tackle scenity with merely scure rhyme schemes. malgamate the biosphere web. he's stinate, which comes across as mensely popular within closure circles. the opposite of bridge music

streperous

subtract snoring. gainsay in the p.m. if you naysay in the a.m. don't roar as you roar. hook and sink, then toggle your rough throat. unisex for the demure. trepidatious schoolboys survey the clout specialists. 'that light was pink, officer!' now liges a kitchen-sink restraining order. the crowd clamours; the 1600 yowl. and every pompous puppy litters forward

tain

pleurisy, but in the planning stages. via laypeople iquitous cuses, the line doctrinates culcation. forget knots. this feathered boa slips to the win column. stricting. a great deal closer to taint than to amnt. some verily. and a boatful of hoven cloves

trusive

to truck to stop to wedlock. bold cheeks. think about the truancy trudge. clusively, pro smothers un. truly we wander aisles and aisles of baby food, mini-whisks, petunia-flavoured crackers, and publican plungers. ob-thrust and ob-threat. versus rustic. how minima!

viate

too flummoxed? well, standably, right? stave on some Persephone sprinkles. forestall any sular aversion when you *lim-in-ate* the abverse. hat's off to artsy spies when they sing in the steam room. go via or go quasi. greyhound forensics vulge multiples of pi. you know, *those* people

out-

landish

in others, that is. full of vetoed landers. not of you-guys birth, so we're
clear (we, that is). dandy is as dandy does. sublimestone parkades; randy
treble clef; practical poetry. when all hell's mancipated. ugh-lish? freakish;
grotesque; queer*ish*

lier

unfastened unbuttoned unzipped from the mainland, one of those domestic
geographies. from the inside voice (inside voice) to the outdoor bench.
even out there, we might bond with the birds: lyre! enter the exits. lapse
into playable hanging fire, all upper case. from god, usually

moded

only in as a grammatical partaker. their past cuckolds them (and: cuckold).
archipelago condoms, modelled on the French. mude and mudier, no
longer. passé composé for the foolscap. annuate a sober diction. forensic
mopeds, everly

rageous

lawlessly well beyond the gross. fifties roller rink with a nineties thumb job. thrust the sweetly horrid against pseudo reruns. *ultra* peri. lights, camera, daction. pinch the popular knuckle, righteously. comments for this thread are now closed. open threads, man. skateboard relics and homo remnants. a bit 'geo'

over-

ly

joyed but also shadowed. past beyond, into super-flushed realms. a Times Roman sudoku, ordinately and orbitantly solved. stump and boozlebam. or boozle. neither cukes nor thinly sliced zucchini. unless yellow and rectangular, less the yellow overlie. minus the revocable 't'

slaugh

looked, nored, then slaaned in the Netherlands, but politely. to unrespect and unglect, refavour another, that cornucopia of cessivity. to hinder the bill, or unbar sand beneath the river. same person always hogging the one-rump toboggan. upturn the premature tooth. genuine redonkery. at times idiom, at times vernaculared Dutch militarism. ample whiles, canned ravioli. to underkill; to overmine

ture

overt opening, viously ambled. sure and tune and ur- and cheer. a doorway to charcoal petals. in the itiate. but not covers. not chorus, nor stripes, nor agreed eyebrow lift. skin swells and nostril buzz. more tonic reboosts. pre-curse that ad, fling nonvites asunder, and sunder the overtrumped sonata. word

whelm

whelping udders while trying to steady the helm. wearing the helpmeet's helmet. while uttering hemmed-in vows. el em en (uh)oh. deuces trump by salute and by overtrouncing. wham

per-

ceíve

adj, adv, n, and other. sight, n. oh, especially sight (cept for the eyes).
then Latin shoved aside the Saxon, sweetly with cussions, and chanced
rocky-road iwinkles. James Baldwin's kaleidoscope mirror. bit player say:
'more at Heave'; you may type *Hoccleve*, you may type his novative plaint

colate

this time a colander, thoroughly trained. I ooze, I leach, I weep. yes, I
filtrate. once in a purple moon; as lively as porous. many eyes, many
needles: passing and simmering though mostly feuds and coffee. bubbling
with a vengeance, two and a half poets scramble thru punctuation

fume

smoked, suasive scents. or wipe away that Spanish smile, this here's patchouli
for nurses! then we meate blooms and blossoms. that rake combs eau de
silence. anyone can fumerize fast-food chicken, if the wind neighbours
the highway. don't forget the acoustics, liquid or otherwise. more aroma,
less stink. more spice, slightly less reek. bue the anchovy with butter and
pomegranate. but stop at cherry

functory

the fungus past desiring participants. a perky dust jacket, a putative dance, a careless touchpad. my hasty thesaurus dorses skimping with the cursor. two breeds apart; one wimp and another impish. foils and foils of mafrost. the mechanical violinist snivels for the uncurious. bat and barstool cartoon it out. because what's worse than a pathy mushroom? thoroughly capable fingers seize the stage, scenes, acts

nicious

pletely woebegonely. duo plicity and begraved trayal. jealous data, custom-made, screening before a live audience. not easily oracular, when the flakes crumble, when the morsels chip. blocks and blocks of flick-picking fili-busters. fidy to your trimental. always a vile, never a ranger. play at nuanced treks till the diurnal's dowry bestows slapstick pirations. you won't laugh, you won't cry

petrate

pletely fathered. criminal Act II, neither avo nor ava. sacred petrol and vernacular cranberry juice. this street kid, with a dash of legend robbery. foul and feathered, every pulled formance. yams more than pumpkins; galactic dust more than Higgs boson, unEarthed. too late to hire more ipheral sonnel. heya, Happy Father's Day, Uncle! il and ishable. cutaneous ish

petuate

not trated, but back-formed and latinate-bulging. nor tinction nor livion, not definitely! a little bit vampire, as in: a bit ic. that gusting pendium. secute from this cisiveness, into a causal memory. yesterday folded into milk crates and mail-slot houses. or stagnant pater missions. every last gerund

spicacious

we bow to sharp anagrams. and to his non-French trepreneurship. wee.
spit and tumble; gift and rumble. chockablock capacity, spired by spirational
paperbacks. acute mental or visual, but no aural info. ad-noun ahoy! flat-
earth morphology strives for a scrambled cipice, for a peated spicacity.
warm underarm secretions – with keen TV cumen – ruse, vade, and jure
this minted tea. swelter next

vasive

before or after vamoose. sonable garlic further to French kissing. the
tensity of visual orthodoxy. way, *way* below the water mark. the film tains
frequent bad language. slap the dramatic sonae when they lineate opera
for kids. watercolours, nursery rhymes, and melancholy buses. even when
twin zygotes aerate, the picture tickles. drip-drip

post-

al

not just verbed joke but slang diagnosis. the late postulant postulates after betting the kinetic ranch. unwild horses and a badass posture escort syntax. and mortems. never quisitions

ed

more than feminist leitmotif. form-element: behind, or: hind. oranges for a sweetly tooth, prior seeds, humed and ever datory. stationary weekly pledges wooden speed. imperil-then-rest. counter with cockcrow lutions. fixed blotch. ever-afterly

erior

superior hindmost. toward the rear of a congress. or any gress. awkward hoity-toities. chronological alphabet, by epoch? botany and upper lips. fundament, stern (can-can), keister (and bum-bum). tush-tush? no, later! dorsal spines. hooligan with an eff. a plus. and a minus

erity

all those begattings, but when will the spring, the geny, the scions do
something for *HIM*? such a bevy of fruit, spawn, and other antebellish
chimera. first known usage: after every century. 'Atlantis says: HI!' good
times, forthcoming

humously

the last, last error. motivated by burial. an afternoon of asundering vowels
and pie whimsy. not so funny now, what? er ... um ... it ... soil, more than
bread and cheese. poned piano positions. I mean it: haste and haster. er

pre-

dilection

before you choose love. one peppermint leaf, two rosy tetrahedrons. steep and steep that dandelion root; Windsor-grown, Ottawa-buffed. naughty directions escort pendant penchants. a dildo of an election. throughout his mother's hexen trials, Kepler peditiously fixed his quiries on harmonic theory. all for her imitable smile. use your chorus. first the toothpick, then the telephoto lens

hensile

after you choose love. always mention the tail, then the mind. your prejectives herald your renouns. hence the crepancy between your forefinger and your thumb. slip into the lingual, praise be. not just tricate monkey tails, but elephant trunks and giraffe tongues. each one of my fingers, and some of yours

liminary

findings and trials and geography homework. every horizon looms with mock invectives, synthetic syntax, taxed at the level of the subsection. twirling only feels better at the line breaks. listing at the thresh of toe and templative quells. make way for liminal exits, luminous trapdoors. sumptuous, I reckon

monition

afore the monitor. usually unembraced. but with tidbits of silver splinters. that's Mama mei-mei. mention the scient. vigilate the miniscence. trace a sketch of a shadowy boding. his or yours? view more comments

ponderance

get ready to weigh in pounds. ready, set, woo. foxtrot of the syllables; muse inside the disco ball. definitely not my second rodeo. free bribes. not since Rome and its remedy for residual stepmothers. and not through questions

posterous

quite a dicament. body-shots beget cucumber-kumquat shots, and then we're all 'right as my right leg' to sum up. to encumber a précis sentence. like poster for cool shade in winter. canopy pairs. and blue texting

stigious

from whence: stidigitation. to dazzle while to blindfold. then fold contigually. high semblance from low uberance. stick it to 'em! their nutritional study hugs versifying. with parallel cision. hocus-hokum. gratiate the fix

varicate

bubbling over. low-church viations and viancies. quibbling for England, for the back alley, for the misled moose. bowlegged coffee tables and knock-kneed tricycles. another bent spine, this one beforehand. false knuckles or shuffling soul, which? contact the medical us, below. scoot, then edit. presume. now go meet the experimental physicist. don't ask pros & cons

still within the logue, this duction *against*

vs. gress

my bable clivity and pensity toward curls
how gressive! the digal son nounces

how easy to pagate a fabulation
bros *after* pros:

leptic

but not just any tuberance; they followed tocol
this here pickups a sperous antonym

over digious sections; fundity over fiteer
evenly, the home secretary vided

lattes and the mis(s)e of phylactic acrobatics
longed and moted
nunciation and truding paganda. liferate nominal

moderately catenate *for*

does not d(r)one niption fits
all the best ways to tribute, rather than spire

how temptible your cern for the gregation
now a certed genial effort

tranyms

first we cur, then demn
for broken records that play on formity

fetti over dolence; jugal over sequences
tradictory carriages. servative and secutive

verge here
trary to public hiking, the tortionist sistently maroons
poetic ceits, spiracies, and fluence

vs. cession

that makes me spicuous, fused, futed when
amphibian anatomy solidates all clusions

doms stantly geal and fer

awesomely

cept, cepter, ceptual

volunteers cede, or assumably

force baking tips solingly into the mix

tenders fectionary ditions

what gruence your jecture relaxes
then volutes the guppy's cenration

present belief pulsion (*im* not *re*), so
minent sody tracts

venance to cure the ficiency. whereas fanity

sucks

that's cephalic of you, emphasis on letarian

voke the ceedings, or feasibly

surprise

our fessor, who's not exactly a per testant

s

o learn to hibit all jections
crastinate till the phesy opts

their digy is my praetor

his viso, her wess

aloof pinquity likes miscuous ximity
you spect then duce

secure every posal, without the usual bation
in order: selytize, fligate, mulgate

more than ductive, the beach menade perly tects

uniform yet blematic
you ponder the sthetics, tein added

gratulations!

vocate cowardice

just when densation escalates to diments
the book flaps your fidant

vs. fessor

which neck trols crackle or sound
which bones fiscate mauve mochas

coct, forms an elaborate crete

because we ceal within centric triangles
you ciliate, fide to the fidential rector

every boscis relies on cedural bability

sider

your tegee loiters portionally
these phetic chats

more than vulsion, a cise recap
these cons picture more

their saic end volunteers prioception
definitely clitic!

don't clusion; y'know?

re-

buttal

plunge driftwood, then back yourself into a bushier and bushier corner. as in: hale and robust quarrel. or when she claims we're in the midst of some sort of clairvoyant naissance. black-and-white mnants, pink taters, and a piebald diva on the side. you might want to rebutter that toast; oh, that's such an elephant!

dundant

waves and waves of. petitive aliens for. this job no longer options you as. withholding when. munerate or imburse if. dunk then bank. dunk then bank. concile times squared with. a merger is a merger is a propos. forgo wavy swishy collars because. how very

frain

fran and stan and parades. curb your doing, your trained beak. then break out those bird songs, break any stentions or vations. vibe-vibe-vibe, imbibe. fraught, tainted, and dicted. piping the long tube of nest, within. if only without. if actually withal. furthermore, templating wit

gurgitate

petitious grrr gyrates through a Yeats finale. how many times can nation-
duty claim the iteration? a skeuomorph × 180, qualing a flood times again.
yes, gain foreign surges and enlargings. or largings

prehend

an app for this appre. ively. 'sthat what's not going well in Spanish? in
Slovenia? dig out the hensile then prepare to hand 'er over. right after that
brusque sprouts burp. heeeeere's the body! a truly pooped plot. beware the
ides of merchandise. I bring you a preamble, a saline 'aha,' a headstone.
rephrased St One

tard

trochaic; circa 1401
not tardy; always tardy; but faithful capitalism: pączki-flavoured sorbet
corpus gets dignant about which noodle-goof slams Asgard brakes
who say harsh and handy? who say
a link and a missing ink blot? who say a tad
a tree bard, othershrewd sumption? rogatory quarter-wit plus comic-boob
clude more, dain less
the boy across the alley; the girl who volunteered at K-Mart nursery; your
    priest's sister; my teacher's nephew; nobody, ever
juvenate the bygones cuz, uh, how many times must you slur they?
only indehiscents blunder phonemes into coconuts. sume sesame seeds
dolted in olive oil and sea salt, pinch of dunce, then a slackeninged
ured to:
'monkey turd, cooties, snot-face, slobber-monster, fatso, flatso, *moroff*';
circa 1956

or:
iterately

over and over, I'm calcitrant about quiring all thinkable sults, every ceipt a collectible. file them cessively, never quite cuperate any losses, then evitably gretting every garded covery. forget the emptive medy: you try to habilitate and habilitate me, but lemon pips lentlessly land in the back alley. my peated bellion juvenates and kindles, cipient of printed acceptance speeches, but with the mighty logo dacted. I'm a cidivist, a cented cluse, due to my curring morse and my nunciated joinders. I'm silient; I'm luctant to nounce. I'm ceptive to jection, specially when my feelings come maindered, to taliate would be unciprocal, but sistance is futile. just say it, don't spray it. glug, glug, glug. how many times must I strongly fute the storative mini-golf course? your readulterated tiger lilies verberate; each furbished spirator, blue or pleated. not enough neging?

whisper to gister yesterday's maple syrup venge; I'll peal your jawline sinuations, with batted shoulders I'll inforce some welcome lief. pistons, rods, and weeping mulberries. dont scind your ardour, verse your world. rant. waive the primands and skip the proaches. your arm braces cascade pugnantly, at least with more fugee borders in mind. my mind. press the proof, then dabble in corporeal volution. rise in the morning, set at twilight. but which sister? the list so far: cleave as a noun, sibling connaissance, the squished coal under our names, a damp pill-popper, much vised spoken syntax, ASL ramps, paraphrase for everyone, trans and for nobody. okay, okay, but the ckoning puter kind of genius. this helping hand. this gressive taliation. do you really want to count 'dneck'? *really*? feasibly, the joke's troactive, just keep 'em keeping. buke, kneel, then sonate. no time for tiree stitution, or to novate the gistrar's thrust, moolah's the ruly hitch: spect, scue, then spite. a feather tickles, a prick floods. member this: demption comes laxed. true, there's never enough time for surrection. but wither the dolent matozoa? click here if you are a gular customer. her first patriation favoured the mote shooting stars. one by one. her second slow-lane tribution verted from the off-centre navel toward the magnet heart. heat of the jiffy. my pertoire lingers as a barren velation. nix the vival, procure a globule of vulva-d vulsion. verily, verily. fuse signation! pudiate the sixties lounge velator. aint no dreamboat verie. I gots to be I. you're the first sponder, the ticent telepath, the upholstered ification. eleven evergreens, two tunnels, six guitar cases, ninety-four languages (Windsoria, 2011). divine my local 'ab' gain. tain the background check. fer for medial medical. that's right, swallow up. but *do* cognize this: when we languishly linquish our splendent babble, we cruit the darling pulsives. who says I'm silient every other week? who plans this copious prieve? just nod. every time you plenish the witty partee, you suscitate my putable quiem. you sume, you plant legumes – did they used to grow quisite? under whose raspberry quisition? and with this tin bucket? in Saskatoon, I'm not sponsible; I'm not verent, but I do lish cinnamon apples. no mandate for straint. you monstrate, he monstrates, they monstratively. every time

trans-

actional

root through? be sure to thank a friend! do you prefer the marriage or the business blend? thru the entire phone call? rational and fluential actress? would you abandon these initials if they spelled out each one of your ad libbed cendents? would you?

cription

mogrify the vestite, then sire the vailing credo. a peccable ripple that scribbles the literate into poetic parency. especially music; especially linguistics. biological since the sixties. obfer or meta lations? the epi ministers to the logue. which is what the page feels like

lucent

tale. seawater, soy milk, sewers. permitting literary subterfuge, but not ingrown disguise. a finicky lover; a phlegmatic leftover. to see clearly, in order to thwart foreseeing clearly. plant a few subs, and you've got: sidy, stantive, and terraneous. just *guise*

un-

beknownst

vulgar suffix, unduly noted. undo, unmake, undead. the most infreely and unwidely lific. spread toward the untoward. quivocally unfriended. quote, finale quote. the sung hero had to unthink his requited love. at last: ravelled

couth

blending with mouth with ounce with cuss. the ruined porn of a six-finger concerto. three paths to flappable iquity, count on the cover story, the tenth inning, still counting. beware of ungrasping, of the uncaught, of outh place

scathed

to not upcoriate harshly and in the past tense. scornful and risive trick luggage scaled to backscratch in passive voice. act caterwaul. berate with a condom. bloody waste of an enigma machine. click here to follow Alan Turing. dismultiplied attention. last time. last time, for sure

under-

handed

reptilian baseball. not left, nor right, not even centre-focus. you can't mean ceptively, a beacon and a shiitake, travelling debauched, or bauched basketball travelling. not underboard or abovely. her feverish pitch. often standable for kids. bent and foxed

ling

dearing suffices wet print diminutively. low, lost, linked. paper ships melt at water leaps. bend over, bend under. every underordinate never forgets the cog-dog rhyme. plunder and blest second fiddle, second banana, second string, first flunky. helpmeets fling. usually, Saturday's comic strip features second-wave lips. parted. ding-a-linging

neath

opposed to super (man, boy, cape). the subcutaneous clit, re-recently cavated. earthbound and sweaty. buzz in the vulva of the spirit world. intone every (double) souciance. cast-off nautical hierarchies. jauntily. cuntily. adverbly. ventually hiding her adorned ding-dong

pinnings

masonry, actually. pluralled wall around the cinct. *guess the correct riposte and collect a sharp verb!* how very undermining of you. warped bedrock and shale woofing. pinterested? the bulwark of his firmation formed the mattress of that arrest. sheep droppings bedeck the meadows, tweak obtained winnings. faved logical position, surreal but why not? unveil some nixed waffle surreality

whelm

over undered. tow and dog, guesstimate and reapproximate. the bear slips into the sage brush unspoken. jocular unwriting. the bearing sister, the achieving brother. unfractions nosedive to subcellars. an almost contranym. such canny thoughts. to fail to imperative; to hold stalwart; to hug the title. now: hoody-winks

up-

chuck

a larf a minute. proud to flarf in the cornflakes. don't tickle, but hurl, then skedaddle before twilight. throw in gurgitatis, toss those informal chunks, gag me with a spork, then grock me. please, donut heaval

heaval

uppity-ly-mobile. braid that fuffle. with reference to vulsions. and the occasional ebullience. and so the earth's crust instanced upward ward. yet another geology. and another. tomorrow's claws miss all that turbulusion. not in a teapot, nor this hullabaloo, nor the theistic uprising. *still and drag*: effulgent, thus bulging

roariously

actamundo! upward stirring motion: left, to under. haiku on a bender. high-larious thermometer. circus for jugglers – go for that! bubble up and vestment down. be ripped. only askance. best seat in the dynasty; outfit to acquit. misfit culprit absconds with various sanskrits. no, not very yogic. abscamalutely, what a chucklehead

sadaisy

irregular widdershins, or a dulterated lackadaisement? that a doohickey
or a vampire hickey? sort through leeway columns, and whoop-de-do
mirth. out of cahoots, so balderdash. upsode-dine and one-angled epsilon.
nonce oodles. hyper-fuddled, backward tip-toeing, flabbergasted, quag-
mirish chicanery. kinky-kooky [also: kookie], and then some wacky
[Britishly: whacky] balderdash. poppycock, agog with gobbledygook and
retro brellas. begunked and ruffled. 'shika-shika, hauh-hauh' goes the
scallywag. so futured

prorogued

crobat

corner piece of the puzzle cries cowboy philosophy. summit + diabetes: ninja-baseball as an ethical example. now *here's* where spelling should matter. muse vs. muse

trocity

humming into anabaptist yoga. oh, that bundant monster metaphor. that fire cavity. that kitschy sund and foamula ebriations. triple eyesores. swapped anapest. an awfully true git. use omnipotence. use à trois. use a tortoise. rent against buy

hoove

to bray about the obvious rooves over their heads. behaeve! befit fits. you'd do well to beheave unicorns, but do not belittle the aquatic campus. no glossy crops, just domestic mons and ters. aloe vera for the misty-brained. it would, you know, suit Swift's vantage, if only to tray the trothed. lastly, be sure to jingle, reprove with aloove

zarre

to bazaar. or, a fit of handsome anger. or bearded. double-guard the bivouac, I'll french ya some Portuguese. etymologically speaking, Mr. Miz. 12 thru K and then biology lectures fluently. c'mon! anyone with football-player lips launches a pucker. lunches with five zany turkeys in the middle of ballet box springs

pacetic

to slang and sling again; 'from my parents, seventy years ago'; to Bojangles jazz, to lure in Cajun, to coy with Chinook. just ducky, and a tad hunky-dory. whyn't dwell local? whyn't Calloway's k-? erg, don't Copacabana. no blade of the guillotine, this, nor a Slavic fable, just good ol' plain peace in a podcast

yote
[*another cartoon insert, here*]

undrum

to not music 1590s slang. pun offers remedies for Oxford riddles. purple chicken teasers. dubious head-scratcher. three times out of five, the answer itiates patois. in correctest English, pedants vote for multiple conundrae. what buttered philological bacles

irgardless

quite irredemptive of vital opposites. ur-blizzard that circulates a worser blunder than deboning. guard the lesser language; irrepeat the legal chestnuts. comic radio for the oral outlaw. embrace fernal and carious and unique. this wake for the dearly body, but so's to parade and brandish limp candy. theretofore: *irregard* irrecuperates

snickety

perhaps vexcessively, almost particularly. or judiciously snobbish. snip-snip-tiny-breeches. concorde pear peels; 'my husband, whom is Irish.' oil-spill niceties snack on the pursuance of lakeshore wine. no whingeing, either. to hoard pet earwax and solid baby oil. to reproach palm leafs wafting near the fedora. inside-out

dulate

wavy and the edge and markedly. undue, undernings, undone. a fly blinks when the room shuffles, when the cape wands, when the sneeze repeals. to think severe volume, not pitchforks. to think fluctuatedly. kempt the flip side of the flippant. called-for handsprings and markable sinuations. pacing, pacing, pacing. *sundheit*

klempt

'okay, do you mean *kempt?*' overcome with germanic overcoming. pounding the hapax. but, what's a veranda? to blubber onto you: verily, verily. listing: struction, versal, something-something-something. minus pletion. plus uncurb. minus unaffixed ballyhoo. plus nine dexed

acknowledgements

Eternal thanks to Susan Holbrook and Louis Cabri for editorial feedback, longed-for criticism, and astute pen marks all over the page.

Over the years, many have given me incredible comments on my writing, offering engrossing conversations, and providing exceptional insight and encouragement for this project. As always, this literary-minded community nourishes and sustains me. For ongoing poetics discussions, I gratefully thank: Michael Barnholden, George Bowering, Colin Brown, Pauline Butling, Louis Cabri, Margaret Christakos, Wayde Compton, Michael Davidson, Maxine Gadd, Susan Holbrook, Susan Holloway, Robyn Laba, Melanie Little, Donato Mancini, Rob Manery, Rolf Maurer, Bridget MacKenzie, Daphne Marlatt, Suzette Mayr, Pamela McCallum, Roy Miki, Jay MillAr, Hazel Millar, Laura Moss, Harryette Mullen, Nancy Newman, Marian Penner Bancroft, Meredith Quartermain, Peter Quartermain, Renee Rodin, Christine Stewart, Catriona Strang, Jacqueline Turner, Fred Wah, and Lissa Wolsak.

Versions of some of the poems in this book appeared in the following literary venues: Gregory Betts and Derek Beaulieu published a few of the 'auto' poems in their *Avant Canada Box*; Lea Graham published earlier 'ad' poems in the Boo's Hollow series of *Atticus Review*; Brook Houghlum published some 'bi' poems in *The Capilano Review*, and Brook Houghlum and Daniel Zomparelli published a version of 'pros & cons' in *The Capilano Review*'s web folio, ti-TCR; Karl Jirgens published a selection of the 'mis' poems in *Rampike*; and Rob McLennan published the chapbook *Ins & Outs* with above/ground press. To each of these editors I am tremendously appreciative and thankful for the opportunity to share my writing.

Early readings from this project happened because of the good work by the following talented and hard-working people: Catherine Bates (for the Yorkshire Network for Canadian Studies) in Leeds; Wayde Compton (Lunch Poems series at SFU) in Vancouver; Kevin McNeilly (Play Chthonics at UBC); Jordan Scott (People's Co-op) in Vancouver; Jacqueline Turner and Rita Wong (Capilano and Emily Carr Universities); and the Margin Shift collective (Gregory Laynor, Robert Mittenthal, Laura Neuman, David Wolach, Jane Wong, and Maged Zaher) in Seattle.

Massive gratitude to Laurie Frick for the cover image: it never ceases to re-whelm!

Finally, I wish to recognize the profound skill, talent, and dedication of the entire Coach House team: Alana Wilcox and Heidi Waechtler for providing incredible edits and noticing all the right (and wrong!) things on the page, and for book design extraordinaire; Veronica Simmonds and Taylor Berry for valuing what lives beyond the page; Jeramy Dodds for his approval via wild percentage grade; and Susan Holbrook for being the best damn editor a poet could ever want or hope or expect or dream to get lucky enough to have as her primary, perpetual, and (pen)ultimate reader: a million, trillion THANKS. Working on this book with such a stounding and ffulgent team has been ceptional and truly lightful!

about
the
author

Nicole Markotić is a poet, novelist and critic. Her poetry books include *Bent at the Spine* (BookThug, 2012), *Minotaurs & Other Alphabets* (Wolsak & Wynn, 1998), and *Connect the Dots* (Wolsak & Wynn, 1994); her novels are *Scrapbook of My Years as a Zealot* (Arsenal Pulp Press, 2008) and *Yellow Pages* (Fitzhenry & Whiteside, 1995). She won the bpNichol Poetry Chapbook Award in 1998, and was nominated for the Stephan G. Stephansson Poetry Book of the Year Award and for the Henry Kreisel First Book of the Year Award. She edits the Wrinkle Press chapbook series and teaches creative writing, children's literature, and disability studies at the University of Windsor.

Typeset in Amethyst.

Amethyst is an old-style type drawn by Jim Rimmer for his Pie Tree Press in New West-
minster, B.C. Rimmer based the idea on a set of roman capitals he drew in 1994 under the
title Maxwellian, which were not released for commercial use but rather as a private type
for his press. The letterforms are a product of Rimmer's calligraphic touch, much in the
same light as his Albertan family.

Printed at the old Coach House on bpNichol Lane in Toronto, Ontario, on Zephyr Antique
Laid paper, which was manufactured, acid-free, in Saint-Jérôme, Québec, from second-
growth forests. This book was printed with vegetable-based ink on a 1965 Heidelberg
KORD offset litho press. Its pages were folded on a Baumfolder, gathered by hand, bound
on a Sulby Auto-Minabinda and trimmed on a Polar single-knife cutter.

Edited by Susan Holbrook
Designed by Heidi Waechtler
Cover photo: *Quantify-Me* at Marfa Contemporary, by Laurie Frick. Photo by Laurie Frick.
Author photo by Louis Cabri

Coach House Books
80 bpNichol Lane
Toronto ON M5S 3J4
Canada

416 979 2217
800 367 6360

mail@chbooks.com
www.chbooks.com